I0488776

Twenty Questions About Incapacity Planning

2018 Edition

Douglas. E. Koenig, Esq.

Copyright © 2017 Douglas E. Koenig
Law Offices of Douglas E. Koenig, PLLC
2530 Meridian Parkway, Suite 300, Durham, NC 27713

All rights reserved.
ISBN: 1522826009
ISBN-13: 978-1522826002

The Publisher and Author make no representations or warranties with respect to the accuracy or completeness of the contents of this work and specifically disclaim all warranties, including without limitation warranties of fitness for a particular purpose. No warranty may be created or extended by sales or promotional materials.

The advice and strategies contained herein may not be suitable for every situation. This work is sold with the understanding that the publisher is not engaged in rendering legal, account or other professional services. If professional assistance is required, the services of a competent professional person should be sought. Neither the Publisher nor the Author shall be liable for damages arising here from use of any information in this book.

The fact that an organization or website is referred to in this work as a citation and/ or potential source of further information does not mean the that Author or Publisher endorses the information the organization or website may provide or recommendations it may make. Further, readers should be aware that the internet websites listed in this work may have changed or disappeared between when this work was written and when it was read.

DEDICATION

This book is dedicated to the many clients I have served and have had the great pleasure to know.

CONTENTS

WHY THIS BOOK?

We are all getting older.

Some of us **like** that thought ... it means being able to vote for the first time, or to go off to college. Or to serve our country in the military.

Getting older might mean the entry to new and exciting things.

For others of us, getting older is a scary thought. It brings images to mind that we simply would prefer to avoid. Sickness or hospitals, being cared for, having others make decisions about where we live and what we can do.

Aging forces us to confront our own mortality.

It is uncomfortable. We stick our heads in the sand.

*Aging forces us to confront our
own mortality.*

How do I know this?

My name is Doug Koenig, and I help people age with their dignity intact. I'm an attorney in Durham, North Carolina, with a law practice that focuses on the needs of elders and their families.

We provide peace of mind. We help people plan for getting older. We can help you too!

I'm not just another attorney.

Growing up in a military household, we were accustomed to the lifestyle of a serviceman. Dad was a Naval Aviator, and we spent time in some of the bases along the Gulf Coast.

I appreciate their sacrifices and I respect the men and women and families that make up our military.

Educated at Dartmouth, and then as an engineer at the Thayer School of Engineering, I know about sweating the details and planning too.

You can't build anything, much less a fighter plane or a bridge, without planning and thinking about the moving parts.

Later in my career I moved into computers and the IT world. I worked with Digital Equipment, and then Ford Motor Company. Some of the work was international, so I learned how cultures and beliefs can affect planning.

Managing parts of many projects, large and small, I

learned how to plan and to prepare for changes and detours and the unknown.

Being a Mediator (and certified in North Carolina) provides an essential understanding of compromise and agreement. Plans usually include some of both, especially when people are involved!

*Planning is preparing
for what you don't
anticipate.*

A key truth I learned is that you can prepare reasonably well for what you see coming ... the harder part is preparing for what you don't anticipate.

Did it apply to me? Yes, it did!

Over time, I noticed that was no longer the young one in the crowd, and that I wasn't really wanting to work at a high-pressure job like I had when I really was younger. But, I didn't plan for change.

Ford reduced workforce expenses and they offered me an opportunity to retire early. This I did not expect... and had not planned for. My kids were grown up and out of the house with directions of their own. After working through the details, and planning options, my wife and I decided to accept.

All the decisions we made as part of that event were based on prayer and thoughtful consideration, and on good solid plans.

Following retirement, I wanted to help other people. After all, I now had the time!

Many options presented themselves, including church, volunteering, and, surprisingly, Law School. Investing in my own future through education was part of the plan and proved the best alternative.

After opening my own practice and working in general law, my mother faced surgeries and my wife's mother began to show signs of aging too. These changes called me into the field of "Elder Law" which is an area of practice dedicated to the needs to our elders and their families.

And, now I include Veterans in my planning too.

We work with families.

It begins, in our practice, with a family meeting as we begin to understand you and your family.

We like to know who you are, and what goals and wishes and dreams you have. No, this is not typical for an attorney, but then, you already know that I'm not your typical attorney.

Once we have the big-picture, we can look into the

details. Whether it is planning for estates, or charitable giving, or retirement, or your health, we have tools and knowledge that can help you.

*Elder Law usually involves
planning. A lot of it!*

Why can I help you?

First, I know what I'm talking about.

Everything I talk about is a real event or story I gleaned from my clients or my own experiences as a Navy brat or a civilian that helps me relate to your stories.

Second, I want to help you.

I didn't stay retired. I opened a practice aimed at elders and their needs. My staff and I want you to age gracefully and with dignity. We can help you with that.

Third, I'm right there with you.

Thinking about your own retirement? Worried about your aging parents? Concerned about your troubled children? I am too. I get it. I can help you.

I wrote this book as part of a series I call "Twenty Answered Questions" about common issues in Elder Law. There might be more than twenty questions, but you get the idea!

Read on, let's get started learning about "Planning for Incapacity."

INTRODUCTION TO PLANNING

What was the most recent plan you made?

Did you travel recently? Did you have lunch with a family member? Did you get up in time to get to work, or to church?

Did you set aside time to read this book?

People plan things with their lives all day long.

If you traveled, you have to know the dates you want to go, and the schedules for airplanes or trains. You have to be ready with your ride or a taxi in time to get to the airport. You have to have tips for the bag handlers, and know where you are going. You have to make it to the plan or the gate on time, with the right boarding pass.

And, you do it in reverse on the way home.

Planning is an essential part of your life.

You even have to be sure you plan to have enough money to pay the bill when it comes next month.

And, it isn't just as simple as a trip you know about. You also plan for the unknown.

Most people have thought about what to do in the event of a disaster.

For example, some families have a plan for fires and fire escapes. They rehearse the plan with the kids, they update the location of the ladder, and they practice using the fire extinguisher. When the time comes that there IS a fire, everyone knows what to do, and everyone stays safe. Of course, there might never BE a fire! In that case, you might feel that you wasted the preparation time ... but, you didn't!

Every moment you spend planning is a benefit to all concerned.

"Incapacity planning" is much the same.

Incapacity sneaks up on a person.

We help families plan to be ready when the time comes so that someone is ready, able, and prepared to step in for another person who needs help.

Incapacity sneaks up on a person.

PLANNING PROTECTS YOUR FREEDOM

Why plan for incapacity?

Planning for incapacity is like most other planning in your life. When do you make plans in your life?

You plan to be ready for an event. You plan to go to a movie or to dinner. You plan what to do after college.

You plan so when the event happens and it is time to follow the plan, you can do it without worrying about your decisions. You plan so you will have more freedom when the time comes because you are ready to move ahead in a predictable way. The family that planned for the fire could react quickly with each person doing their part.

"Incapacity planning" is much the same. Incapacity sneaks up on a person. Most of us cannot tell when we are losing decision-making capacity. We think everything is perfect and that we are doing fine long after we have started to slip.

Perhaps you have noticed that slight hesitation in yourself or in a loved one, when you can't make decisions as fast as possible. Or, if you make poor decisions, such as when the sure-thing stock purchase wasn't really a very good idea.

Louise was a proud woman. She had cared for herself for all of the thirty-five years since her husband had passed. But, lately she noticed that she had some trouble remembering to pay the bills, and had to make several calls to get those pesky late fees removed. Then, she paid the paper-boy twice in the same month.

What was happening to her?

A plan for reaching out to others will help families plan to be ready when the time comes so that someone is ready, able, and prepared to step in for another person who needs help.

You should plan both for the time when you can't make decisions for yourself, and for the time when a person wants you to help make decisions for them.

When you work with us, we discuss both health care planning as well as financial planning. The tools we most often use are called "Powers of Attorney".

What kinds of things should I plan for?

The kinds of decisions you make on a day to day basis might be related to banking, finance, real estate, health care, treatment plans, and so on.

Louise didn't want to ask for help, but she was a little worried. She didn't want her house to be at risk if she missed a payment, but she also didn't want to admit to anyone that she needed help.

Yes, Louise was proud of her independence. But, she also didn't quite trust anyone to help her.

Not all plans are about mental incapacity or gradual loss of cognitive functions (the "decision-making" ability). Some are more immediate and the effects of incapacity can strike suddenly.

You might have a small business that needs to be run by someone capable if you are unavailable for a time period.

You might have a special needs child that needs care, or an ill spouse … neither of whom would do well if you could not make decisions for them.

Bob was a successful entrepreneur by all standards. He had built his financial planning business over the past six years and had developed a nice clientele of middle income people who depended on his calm and sage advice about the markets and investments. He had a wife and two kids in elementary school.

Then, Bob was in a traffic accident driving to a local conference. He wasn't badly injured, but spent several months recuperating before he could get back to work full time. Unfortunately, some of his best clients had moved on to another firm because they wanted advice sooner than Bob was able to provide it.

Bob was incapacitated, even if just for a few months. Could Bob have prevented this loss of clients through planning?

And, whom would Bob have named to help in a time of crisis? Would that person have been ready to step in to manage the business for Bob? Proper planning is not just naming your agent, but making sure the agent will be able to function as you wish.

---

*Planning goes both ways ... you plan for when you can't make decisions **for yourself**, and you plan for that time when you might have to make decisions **for another person**.*

POWERS OF ATTORNEY ARE THE IMPLEMENTATION OF YOUR PLAN

What is a Power of Attorney?

A Power of Attorney is a document that confers important powers from one person (the "Principal") to another person (the "Agent").

It can be effective right away or at a future date, and it can expire at some future date or be effective as long as the principal is living.

A Power of Attorney permits the agent to perform a wide range of actions on behalf of the principal. Often, the intent is to confer the maximum authority allowable. The agent is authorized to do nearly everything that the principal could personally do for himself.

DeShalle wanted to sell her house in Michigan now that she had moved down to North Carolina with her family. But, she wasn't able to travel well when her arthritis acted up. She needed a way to let her cousin in Farmington sell the house without her being present.

DeShalle asked an attorney to draw up a limited Power of Attorney that gave her cousin the right to act as her "agent" and sell the house for her. The cousin could only sell the house and transfer the funds to her bank account. The power he had as her Agent expired once the sale was completed.

She also had her daughter listed as her agent under a durable general power of attorney in North Carolina. Her daughter could not act until DeShalle lost capacity to act for herself, but once that happened, DeShalle would receive the financial help she needed to manage her affairs.

A power of attorney is a document that confers important powers from one person to another person.

Are There Different Kinds of Powers of Attorney?

Attorneys usually work with two kinds of powers of attorney: financial, and health-care.

Financial powers of attorney deal with banking and money issues. Medical or health-care powers deal with care issues, medications, admissions and so on.

The following are some key characteristics of all powers of attorney.

- A Power of Attorney (Power of Attorney) can be general, granting "all" powers defined in North Carolina statutes, whether for health care or financial concerns.

- A Power of Attorney can also be a specific power that authorizes the agent to act for a specific purpose. Some Power of Attorney documents have time limits.

- A "durable" power means it continues to allow the agent to act even if the principal cannot make decisions for himself.

- "Immediate" powers means the powers take effect immediately when signed; "Springing" power means they take effect when the principal loses capacity.

A third kind of Power of Attorney is the "Living Will" or as it is more correctly named, the "Advance Directive."

The Advance Directive document also gives instructions in advance to medical professionals as to how you wish to be treated at the end of your life.

Related to this is the "DNR," or Do Not Resuscitate order, which will instruct doctors and EMTs to limit their efforts to revive you if your heart or breathing stop. Lawyers cannot provide this form because it must be prepared with your primary care physician and reviewed by your medical people.

In Elder Law, the most common forms of Powers of Attorney are financial and health-care

---

Is there much difference between Financial and Medical Powers?

Yes, they are very different documents with different powers.

A **financial** Power of Attorney grants financial powers. These usually include typical transactions such as banking and investments, buying and selling of property, or gifting to others. Some additional powers are often important for our clients, such as the ability to create and fund trusts.

A **medical** (or "health care") Power of Attorney grants decision-making powers related to medical care. It is a document that allows a designated person (a "health care agent") to make medical decisions for an individual if he or she is unable to make such decisions for him/herself.

Carole had a family history of early onset dementia. She wanted her husband to make financial decisions for her if she ever had capacity problems. She had an attorney complete a durable financial power of attorney and record it in the county in which they lived.

When Carole had an unexpected stroke, her husband was able to take care of her IRA, make reasonable stock trades, and keep her small business bank accounts and credit cards in order.

At the same time, Carole knew that her husband would be unable to make the kinds of medical decisions she wanted. He was too emotional to think straight when his wife was ill ... that was obvious when the babies were born. So, she asked her sister to be her agent under a Medical power of attorney. She knew she could trust her sister to make the difficult decisions Carole would need made for hospitalization and at her end of life.

Carole and her husband planned for one event, and were surprised by a different one. But, because their plan was in place, it was easy to adapt.

Some people ask how extensive these powers are in practice. The agent cannot actually perform medical *procedures*, but are able only to help the principal make decisions for themselves.

In addition to making medical decisions, a Power of Attorney also permits the agent to decide where the principal will live or recuperate if needed.

---

*A **financial** power of attorney grants financial powers, such as banking or selling property.*

Do I lose the right to make decisions once I sign a Power of Attorney or once the agent has been activated?

Yes and no. Under an "Immediate" Power of Attorney, the principal retains all decision-making power. But, even after a Power of Attorney is operative due to incapacity, the principal sometimes can still act for himself or herself. This could depend on what powers have been granted and what decisions the principal wants to make.

The Principal and the Agent have "concurrent authority" to act on behalf of the principal. So, as long as the principal CAN make decisions, they are allowed to. This can be to make independent decisions, or it can be with the help of the Agent.

Under a "springing" power of attorney, the agent does not have any power to act UNTIL the principal is deemed to lack capacity. That usually means that a doctor or a court decides that the principal lacks capacity to act on her own behalf, which allows the agent to take over responsibilities.

> *Generally, the Principal and the Agent have "concurrent authority" to act on behalf of the principal.*

However, the principal DOES lose the right to make decisions if a **guardianship** of the estate is imposed and supervised by the court. In that case, the "ward" (the principal who is now under the guardianship) will no longer be able to act for themselves.

LuAnn had increasing trouble with remembering facts, and that kept her from working, so she quit her six-figure consulting job. Eventually, she developed aphasia (inability to select the right words to say), and was diagnosed with semantic dementia. She was only 40. Her husband, Robert, never had a power to act for her because it just seemed too soon to worry about planning.

Robert had to pursue a guardianship, at a cost of almost $5,000 to gain control over his wife's IRA and bank accounts so they could sell enough to cover the medical bills. They could have avoided this by a simple Financial Power of Attorney.

And, if the principal is making bad decisions (or none) and has been deemed to lack capacity, then the principal will not be able to make decisions on his or her own **until** he or she regains capacity.

Susie denied that she had any trouble with her memory, but her daughter could tell. When she stopped caring for her own basic hygiene, Susie needed real help. She moved to an assisted living facility in North Carolina, but was an elopement risk (she didn't stay at the facility, choosing to go "places" without knowing how to go or return). When she called for an Uber driver to take her "home" to Florida, her daughter invoked the agency granted under the properly recorded power of attorney, and had Susie moved to memory care to control her elopement risk.

Susie was safe and secure, and was properly cared for by her daughter and the staff. Although she didn't like it, it was exactly what she planned for when she gave her daughter the right to make medical and financial decisions for her after she lost capacity.

Regaining capacity may be as simple as recovering from the stroke, or being cleared by a doctor to have capacity to make decisions.

Carl had set up a power of attorney with his brother acting as agent. Carl had a stroke, and was unable to make decisions. His brother acted for him for six months, and when Carl had recovered enough, he was able to retake control over his finances.

I have Alzheimer's dementia. Can I still sign a Power of Attorney?

It depends. An early diagnosis is not a limitation on your capacity. Many of our elder clients have Alzheimer's, and are perfectly capable of making decisions. But, it is a progressive disease, and sadly, your capacity for making decisions will decline.

If you are asking that question, you are probably sufficiently capable of making most decisions. But, if you are asking that as the caregiver for a person with Alzheimer's ... well, that is when we have to rely on our assessment, or on a finding of capacity (or not) by a doctor.

Life and planning for eventualities is a process; whatever diagnosis or illness you have, planning is essential. And, capacity varies from day-to-day, so, it is always a good idea to plan.

You never really know exactly when you will need the plan.

Planning is a process.

NAMING THE RIGHT AGENT CAN IMPROVE THE QUALITY OF YOUR LIFE AS YOU AGE

Who can I name as "agent" in my Power of Attorney?

You can name anyone over 18 who will act with competence when you cannot. Often this is a spouse, or family members. Sometimes it is an entity, such as a corporate trustee or a lawyer. Very rarely an agent can be a neighbor or close friend.

You should always trust your agent because they will make very important decisions for you. If they are not trustworthy, your risk is substantial.

> *You should always trust your agent before naming them.*

Additional rules apply to naming Health Care agents. A health care agent must be over 18, and cannot be a caregiver or an employee of the caregiver.

There are several points to consider in choosing a decision-maker for health care agent:

- Have I asked this person if he/she is willing?

- Have I talked with this person enough so that he/she understands my preferences, values and goals?

- Will this person follow my preferences, even if they differ from their own?

- Can this person make decisions in sometimes difficult or emotional situations?

You should begin by discussing and deciding on your goals of care in the event of a severe brain injury or other life-threatening illness. And, it is important to be careful in identifying any personal, cultural or religious beliefs that may affect treatment decisions.

Talk about your health care wishes before you name an agent to act for you.

Who decides if I'm incapacitated?

Incapacity can mean many things. Does it include times when the principal is away for an extended period of time, or is missing? Does it mean when an addicted child is under the influence? Does it mean when a person is suffering from the advancement of dementia? Consequently, disputes can arise as to whether the triggering mechanism (i.e., when the principal's incapacity) actually occurred.

Often, it is clear when incapacity starts (e.g., the person has a stroke). But, dementia does not make that transition point clearly evident.

When necessary, a decision must be made. In some cases, the agent can make the decision. We usually suggest this for families who trust one another. In other cases, one or more licensed physicians must make a determination. And in some cases, a court is asked to make a determination of capacity.

Incapacity can mean many things. And, with dementia it varies from day to day.

Law Offices of Douglas E. Koenig, PLLC
2530 Meridian Parkway, Suite 300, Durham, NC 27713

When does a person lose capacity?

Determining this point is touchy for most people.

It isn't "incapacity" when people make decisions we don't agree with. For example, does your teenager make good choices when she chooses her date for Prom? Not all dads agree!

I sometimes call this being "dumb" - but there is no law against poor decisions. You can choose to act different ways that would make no sense to another person under normal conditions. For example, you can choose to stop wearing seat belts while driving. Sure, studies show that people in seat belts survive car crashes better than those who don't. But, you can make that choice because you have "capacity" to decide … even if others might disagree vehemently. And, in this case, even if it is against the law.

What about a person who is drunk? Certainly there is a period of incapacity while they are not sober enough to drive or make decisions … were they "incapacitated" when they poured themselves into the driver's seat? Possibly! The criminal law is for this is usually called "Driving while intoxicated", but it could be driving while "incapacitated!"

It is the same for temporary incapacity caused by anesthesia during surgery, age (under 18), or even being out of the country when a decision needs to be made by you. These are all kinds of "incapacity."

But, that isn't usually what people are talking about when they wonder about "losing capacity."

Instead, when your mom makes irresponsible decisions that are a failure of judgment, she will have a possible case of incapacity.

Note, this is when dad makes a decision that has possible consequences affecting his physical or financial health and he cannot see the effects or risk.

That is the executive reasoning (or lack thereof) that we look for in a determination of incompetence or in lacking capacity.

Often doctors must make this decision for us. And, a financial Power of Attorney will usually spell out when and who has to decide. Doctors look for executive decision-making ability.

Several tests are used to help with the decision, and you may have already had these. One is sometimes called the "Mini-Mental State Examination" (MMSE) and is used to make an initial determination of capacity with a very few questions.

Others involve eye-hand coordination, including drawing of a clock. None of these is perfect, but each will provide a glimpse into the person's mental state and be a data point in the decision about incapacity.

So, don't fear this step because it is really a protection for you... making poor decisions because you *want to* is your choice, but making dangerous decisions because you have lost capacity means that you need help and protection.

Why do I need a document? Can't I just tell my daughter to make decisions for me?

You can tell her, but it is likely that won't be enough for most decisions she would need to make.

> *Phyllis wanted her youngest daughter, Mary, to assist her as she aged and when she needed help. But, Phyllis didn't execute any documents.*

> *When her daughter wanted to withdraw funds to cover a medical bill, then bank refused. Then, the other children got involved, and no one could agree on how to help or what to do. Eventually, the family had to go to court to resolve the fights, and Mary was not named the guardian.*

Is that what Phyllis wanted? Of course not.

In the absence of a validly appointed agent under a recorded Power of Attorney, only a court-appointed guardian has the authority to make financial and business decisions on behalf of the principal.

Waiting until it is too late might mean an expensive process to get a court involved. And, then, you might not like the person appointed to be the guardian. It is always better to have the documents in place before they are needed.

OTHER TOOLS FOR PLANNING

Powers of attorney are the most common tool to assist with planning for incapacity.

Are there other ways to have a person help me make decisions?

Yes. There are many tools used to guide others as to your wishes. Some simply state decisions you have made; others allow trusted people to help.

For example:

- A Last Will and Testament tells people your wishes after your death. This is a specialized document that will be too late to help you while you are living. Wills can be used to direct your assets into trusts (which have their own rules), or to give ("devise") real property (houses or land) to others.

- Trusts (*Living, Irrevocable, or Special Needs*) can support incapacity planning as well, and the "Trustee" (the person assigned to manage the Trust assets) performs in a similar role as the Agent. A Trust serves a similar purpose to

Powers of Attorney because it lets the trustee make decisions with the assets in the Trust. In some cases, you can be the trustee of your own Trust. Trusts absolutely require the help of an attorney.

- Owning assets jointly is another way to control decisions … Joint Ownership of assets (*a high risk*) can include different kinds of ownership, including Joint Tenancy with Right of Survivorship, Tenants in Common, or Tenancy by the Entireties. Bank accounts or investment accounts can be owned in some of these ways, and some bank accounts can have a Pay-on-death ("POD") provision.

- In a very broad sense, even Gifts can be a form of decision-making delegation, although you probably will *lose control of assets*.

There are many ways to get help when you need it. But, planning the best way for you is essential.

TAKE CONTROL OF YOUR QUALITY OF LIFE - GETTING STARTED WITH POWERS OF ATTORNEY

Where can I get a Power of Attorney?

You can obtain forms from various agencies or on-line. However, we always advise that you use an elder law attorney for a Power of Attorney.

Why should I use an Elder Law attorney for this?

Elder Law attorneys think about different topics and issues than a general practitioner or an on-line form might (not that an on-line form actually "thinks").

For example, we often consider what happen during a period of *incapacity*. Most legal documents or processes assume you have some degree of capacity to *understand* ... such as the "intent" to commit a crime, or the ability to understand right from wrong.

But, in the elder law world, many of our clients or their parents face a time of growing fear of "incapacity," or temporary or permanent loss of the decision-making powers.

We help the family address this issue, including both the powers to be shared and the agents to be chosen. We even offer training for agents so they understand their important roles.

Elder Law attorneys are uniquely qualified to help you plan for incapacity

---

What are the documents I need?

In the most general sense, to be fully protected, you will need the following types of powers of attorney:

- Financial Power of Attorney;
- Health care Power of Attorney,
- An Advance directive for health care, and
- Release of private health information.

Do I only need one kind of power of attorney?

No. Usually you will need all of these, and sometimes, more than one version.

In some cases, we will prepare more than one of the same type of Power of Attorney. This happens, for example, when a principal wants to name one general agent for incapacity, and a different agent with limited powers for day-to-day assistance as their dementia progresses.

Jerry was worried about his ability to make good financial decisions and his son was a financial planner. However, he wasn't ready to turn over all decision making authority to his son. Jerry was able to create a limited power of attorney for investment decisions for his son, and a springing power of attorney for all other decisions. Then, Jerry could be confident that he would retain control over most areas of his life while still giving his son control over his finances at a future point when he lacked capacity.

When clients come to see us for estate planning, we often advise a full financial power of attorney for the agent rather than a springing power. Our reason is simple … if you trust your agent later, you had better trust him now.

Here, we advocated a split power in Jerry's case so that Jerry's son could learn what his dad wanted in all aspects of his life and they could gradually transition control, while Jerry's son had the ability to exert control if necessary. But, it is important to note that this doesn't work for all families. And, it may be an extra risk for people with dementia because one normal feature of dementia may include distrust of others… particularly regarding finances. Planning with an elder law attorney is the only way to be sure all the questions are asked.

Law Offices of Douglas E. Koenig, PLLC
2530 Meridian Parkway, Suite 300, Durham, NC 27713

In addition, we help clients think about health care documents in the same way. We often suggest different people for each type of power of attorney, based on our discussion with our clients and our evaluation with them.

There are several forms of health-care Powers of Attorney, and every state has state-specific guidelines. North Carolina has a legal standard form for the advance directive and the health care power of attorney. There are other forms as well. For example, a form commonly used in our practice is the "Five Wishes" form, developed by a group called Aging with Dignity. This form is available in North Carolina and most other states. It can be used to replace the state standard form, and is written in language that is easy to understand.

What if I don't complete a Power of Attorney?

If you do not have a valid Power of Attorney, your agent will not be legally able to make decisions (within the scope of the granted powers).

So, for example, if your spouse has a stroke, and you have to find the banking instructions to pay the mortgage, an "agent" of the principal would have to call the bank to provide the instructions or to release the payment. If you don't have a valid Power of Attorney, there is no agent assigned to call the bank.

A spouse can sometimes be allowed to act, but it is

within the discretion of the bank or other entity.

If no one has a valid power granted to them as agent, and a decision must be made, then a guardianship will be required. Guardianships are expensive processes and begin with a petition filed at the Clerk of Superior Court.

When should I arrange to make a Power of Attorney?

You should do this **while you are competent** to make decisions. If you wait too long, no one will be able to help you sign this document.

You might also want to ask for help in such areas as running a business or making investment decisions. It is also important to have a Power of attorney when one spouse owns assets in their name alone.

A financial Power of Attorney requires a very high level of understanding on the part of the principal before it can be signed. We do an assessment for all clients before we allow them to sign any legal document.

Most people who can ask the sort of questions posed in this FAQ would be competent to sign a financial Power of Attorney.

How Important is Choosing an Agent?

VERY important!

Be very careful about whom you choose as an agent.

We are very careful about selecting an agent when the agent seems opportunistic or overly eager to serve in that role. If we see this, we will discuss our concerns with our clients.

If there is a risk of family fights about who gets to be the agent, sometimes a guardianship is a better choice because that is supervised by the court.

The same general approach applies to the Health Care Power of Attorney. Any adult who has the understanding and ability to make health care decisions for him/herself may execute a health care Power of Attorney. They may select any competent adult person to make medical decisions for them in the event that they are unable to make those decisions themselves.

Be very careful about whom you choose as an agent. The agent must be trustworthy before you name them.

GUARDIANSHIP – THE LAST RESORT

Do I need an Attorney for Guardianship?

You do not need an attorney, but you probably should have one available. Guardianship hearings can be contentious; the judge will require evidence; and you will need to convince the judge regarding capacity of the person and your ability to manage that person's assets better than anyone else.

An attorney will cost between $3,000 and $10,000 for a typical guardianship, and it takes between 10 and 60 days, normally. If the family contests it, the process can be longer and more expensive.

Jerry had a stroke that left him unable to speak or walk. He and his wife had divorced some years before, and he had never assigned anyone to be his agent under a new power of attorney. He had no will, no trusts, no beneficiaries on his accounts ... nothing that would help others make decisions for him. He had thought about plans for which kids would get his wealth, but never took any legal steps. However, Jerry's ex-wife was still listed as his agent on the properly recorded power of attorney.

When Jerry was through the first 20 days of rehab, he was transferred to a skilled nursing home for his long-term recovery. But, who could sell funds in his IRA to pay for his care? At $10,000 per month, the facility wasn't willing to wait very long, and because he had almost a million dollars in his funds, he could not qualify for any public benefits.

The facility contacted his ex-wife, who notified the IRA fund and started to withdraw to cover his expenses. That is when the trouble started.

Jerry's children immediately started to argue about the level of care, the facility, which state Jerry should be in, and whether the ex-wife could legally withdraw funds at all. The argument eventually got to court, and one of the children filed a petition for guardianship. After 3 months, and $40,000 of Jerry's money, the child was awarded guardianship. She moved Jerry to another state, and his money never went to the kids as he had intended.

This could have been avoided with proper planning.

Once a guardian is assigned, the court will supervise the processes. That will add to the work and scrutiny on the Agent.

Having a valid Power of Attorney can avoid the cost of guardianships.

GAIN CONTROL – UNDERSTAND THE TERMS AND DEFINITIONS

What is the "Principal"?

The Principal is the person who is granting powers to another. Usually this is a spouse or an elder in the family who is planning for changes.

What is an "Agent"?

The Agent is the person to whom powers are granted under a valid Power of Attorney. This applies to all types of powers of attorney.

What does "Durable" mean? How do I know if a document is "Durable"?

A "durable" power means it continues to allow the agent to act even if the principal cannot make decisions for himself. A document is durable if you see one of the following kind of language:

> "This Power of Attorney shall not be affected by subsequent disability or incapacity of the principal"

> or

> "This Power of Attorney shall become effective upon

the disability or incapacity of the principal."

What is a "springing power"?

This is a term referring to the timing for granting of powers. When a principal wants to sign a document now, but not grant powers until a later date, those powers are called "springing".

When does a "springing power" begin?

It depends on the document. "Springing" powers generally begin when the principal is determined to have lost capacity to make certain decisions. The document describes these decisions and when they can be made by another person.

Usually, we advise that the agent be given all the powers available to them for the kind of document (e.g., Financial or Medical) when the principal lacks capacity to decide for themselves.

The powers named can be very specific. For example, a medical Power of Attorney might specify that decisions about admission to a hospital can be made by the agent, but not decisions about end-of-life. Or, a financial Power of Attorney might specify that a particular agent may manage a bank account while the principal is out of the country, but not to manage investments or sell property.

Sometimes springing powers begin at a particular event, or on a specific date.

RECORDING AND UPDATING A POWER OF ATTORNEY

Does my power of attorney have to be recorded?

In general, all financial powers of attorney need to be recorded to be effective. They do not need to be recorded when signed, but may be held until needed. Nevertheless, we advise that the financial Power of Attorney always be recorded once you have completed it. It can't be lost that way, and accusations of fraud are less likely to be raised.

Only when the spouse is named as the agent can the Power of Attorney can be operative without recording. And, that is true in some states including North Carolina, but may not be true in other states.

Financial powers of attorney
should always be recorded

To record a document, the properly formatted document needs to be presented to the clerk of court at the estate division in the county of your residence. There is a small fee.

In North Carolina, the Financial Power of Attorney does not need to be witnessed by additional people, but it must be notarized. The notary seal must be legible, and "pressed" notary stamps are approved by the clerk when presented in person but generally do not work electronically.

If your Financial Power of Attorney document was not notarized in your home state when it was signed, you will not be able to record it in North Carolina until it is notarized. In that case, we always advise that a new document be signed.

The Health Care Power of Attorney does not need to be recorded. However, the Health Care Power of Attorney (and the Advance Directive) should always be given to the doctor or hospital, along with any HIPAA releases for the family.

Can I revoke a Power of Attorney?

Yes, you can!

There are three main ways a durable general Power of Attorney is revoked.

- A recorded Power of Attorney is revoked by the death of the principal.

- You may file a written revocation with the Register of Deeds in the same county.

- An unrecorded Power of Attorney may be revoked by specific written revocation, physical act of revocation, or in any manner specified in the document. North Carolina requires powers of attorney be recorded for all agents who are not the principal's spouse.

Notify third parties when revoking a recorded power of attorney.

You should always tell the agent and all persons or entities relying on the Power of Attorney that you have revoked it. Technically, someone not notified will have no liability for actions they take on the advice of the person they "knew" to be the agent.

When should I update my plans?

Advance care planning is a process, not a onetime event, and your wishes may change as circumstances change. You should review your choices whenever any of the "Decision D's" occur:

- **Doctor**: Review your wishes every time you have a physical exam

- **Decade**: Your 60th, 70th birthday, and so on

- **Death**: of a loved one (or Birth)

- **Divorce**: yourself or a close family member

- **Diagnosis**: Dementia or other progressive illness

- **Decline**: when you (or others) notice a decline in your health

- **Desires change**: As in the case of family estrangements

- **Dedications**: such as gifts or charities

- **Distribution**: such as for an annuity that pays out on a family Inheritance

ACT RESPONSIBLY – WHAT YOU MUST KNOW TO BE AN AGENT UNDER A POWER OF ATTORNEY.

I am an agent under a Power of Attorney. What can I do with it?

That depends on the scope of the powers granted in the document.

You may have a "statutory" form (meaning a form that is part of North Carolina law), which lists generic powers and has the principal initial each one.

Some forms will start with the statutory version and add additional specific powers for certain purposes. For example, our office adds certain trust and gifting language to the form which allow an agent to properly plan for public benefits using trusts.

Other forms are very specific as to the powers they grant. These tend to be very short, listing just the power (such as "Sell my house in Florida") or very long, calling out each power in detail.

Do I have any responsibilities as an agent under a Power of Attorney?

Yes, you must act as a "fiduciary" for a financial Power of Attorney.

That means you have to spend money wisely, or make good decisions, for the benefit of the principal, according to reasonability standards. If you don't, the principal's family may be able to file a legal complaint to have you stop, or be removed, or repay the funds that are being contested.

Your State law will spell out what responsibilities you have as an Agent.

Do I have to act if I am listed as an Agent?

No.

You are not obligated to act. You **may** act, but you do not technically have to act under financial Power of Attorney. If you do not, there is no legal repercussion.

However, if you do act, then you fall under the fiduciary responsibility rules for your actions.

In the event that a guardian is named, that person must act as needed to protect the principal's interests.

A Guardian MUST act on behalf of the ward.

An Agent MAY act on behalf of the Principal.

What is my responsibility as a Health Care agent?

For medical powers of attorney, the rule is generally to make reasonable decisions that do not run counter to known wishes of the principal.

For example, if the principal needs an operation, you should be able to decide where it will take place and when, possibly which doctors can perform the operation, and then authorize repayment via the principal's insurance. You probably cannot elect to skip the surgery, unless there is a persuasive and prevailing religious or personal reason that the principal would not have approved the operation.

Different from the Financial Power of Attorney, the agent under Health Care Power of Attorney is usually expected to act, although still not required to. However, if a health care agent does not act, the hospital and doctors will make the necessary decisions. If the Advance Directive is available, that can guide decisions that would also be made by the Agent under a Health Care Power of Attorney.

What obligations does a third-party have to follow my decisions as an Agent?

Generally, a third party must accept a valid, recorded Power of Attorney. Sometimes, an old, or out-of-state document might not be recognized. But, an agent needing to act on behalf of a principal can often get the Power of Attorney in place and act accordingly if it was recorded.

For a financial Power of Attorney, North Carolina requires signatures to be notarized, although some other states do not. If you have a Power of Attorney recorded in one of those states that is not notarized, it is very likely that North Carolina entities will refuse to honor the Power of Attorney. You can have it resigned, or notarized, or completely redone to fix the problem.

A medical or health care Power of Attorney needs to be both notarized AND witnessed by two witnesses. These witnesses should not be the caregiver or employees of the caregiver. New legislation in North Carolina will allow either notarization OR witnesses, if it passes.

What happens if someone petitions for Guardianship to take over my rights as an Agent?

A guardianship is necessary when there is no agent, or when someone thinks that the agent is not acting with the principal's best interests.

A petition is filed, and there will be a hearing. The judge will listen to evidence, and will decide to grant some, all, or none of the powers requested. Once the guardian is appointed, the court will supervise their actions.

At that same time, your powers as agent will cease, unless the court grants the guardian some of the powers and you some other of the powers. This is unusual.

Once a guardian is appointed, your powers cease and you cannot legally act as the agent. You do not have to notify third parties because the guardian will notify them. This is not a time to squeeze in one more action. Let the process work as it should!

Can I resign as Agent? What happens then?

Yes, you can resign by notice to the principal and/or to the guardian. You should also notify all third parties who were accepting your actions. They will begin to take direction from the new agent or the guardian, as appropriate.

Who replaces me as Agent?

Finding a replacement is not your job, normally. If the document calls out a method to replace the agent, you and the new agent should follow those rules. If there is nothing in the document, state law might be used to define a new agent.

If nothing else, someone would have to petition for a guardianship, which you could do to force the appointment of a replacement. Often a nursing home will file the petition if there are no agents to help them with decisions for the principal.

Douglas E. Koenig, Esq.

ABOUT THE AUTHOR

Attorney Douglas E. Koenig

- Estate Planning
- Medicaid Planning
- Incapacity Planning
- Special Needs Trusts
- Veteran's Benefits (A&A and SCD)

Law Offices of Douglas E. Koenig, PLLC
2530 Meridian Parkway, Suite 300, Durham, NC 27713

I'm a Navy brat, said in the kindest of terms! As a child in a military family, I understand the unique challenges of military life from that perspective. Yes, moving all over the Gulf Coast, making new friends, and having dad deployed for long periods ... it is what we all went through together. And, as a result, I appreciate the sacrifice of those who have chosen to serve in the armed forces.

Most recently, I'm a graduate of the Michigan State University College of Law where I was involved in the business law and alternative dispute resolution programs. The College of Law is an established and accomplished institution in many areas and is a top 100 law school at a Big Ten University.

I completed undergraduate work at Dartmouth College and hold a degree in Materials Engineering from Thayer School of Engineering. My history and prior engineering and business experience contribute a strong foundation to my Juris Doctor, and my service to you!

In 2010, I established a compassionate Elder Law practice, which is focused on four main areas, including Veteran's benefits, Medicaid planning and crisis response, Special Needs Trusts, and Estate Planning and the related wills, trusts, and powers of attorney.

Not everyone can afford legal representation, so when appropriate, I offer time and expertise to various programs, including LEAP (via the NC Bar Association), Legal Aid of North Carolina, the UNC Pro Bono Cancer Clinic, and other organizations. My other service time includes the Durham Downtown Rotary Club and the Gideons.

When we meet, be sure to ask about my work with Digital Equipment Corporation and Ford Motor Company in Michigan prior to locating in North Carolina. I have found connections with my clients through shared work experiences all over the world!

Church matters are important too and so I spend time participating in and leading bible study groups (in case you are invited, Bible Study Fellowship is a wonderful organization!).

I also enjoy sailing, photography, traveling, and, of course, friends and family! This year, my wife and I will have been married for 39 years, and we have three grown children and two grandchildren.

Douglas E. Koenig, Esq.

Law Offices of Douglas E. Koenig, PLLC
http://www.dougkoeniglaw.com -- 919-724-4778

FINAL WORDS

I hope you enjoyed reading this book as much as I enjoyed writing it.

If you would like to pursue planning for incapacity or any other aspect of Elder Law for yourself or for your loved ones, please give us a call.

919-724-4778

If you mention 5WISHES when you call, you will receive a free copy of the Five Wishes form that you can have notarized for free at our office.

The Law Offices of

DOUGLAS E. KOENIG

PLLC

2530 Meridian Parkway, Suite 300

Durham, NC 27713

Douglas E. Koenig, Esq.

.

www.ingramcontent.com/pod-product-compliance
Lightning Source LLC
Chambersburg PA
CBHW071630170526
45166CB00003B/1269